How to Travel Effectively and Joyfully

Explore the World with Ease, Joy, and Confidence

Anna Imrichova

© 2025 Anna Imrichova.

All rights reserved.

No part of this publication may be reproduced, distributed, or transmitted in any form or by any means without the prior written permission of the copyright owner.

Table of Contents

Prologue 6
Introduction 8
Chapter 1 THE PLAN 11
  ✈ Where would you like to travel? 16
Chapter 2 CHOOSING YOUR IDEAL DESTINATION
.... 25
Chapter 3 FLIGHTS 27
Chapter 4 ACCOMMODATION – BOOKING A STAY THAT WILL THRILL YOU! 53
Chapter 5 COMPARING ACCOMMODATION PRICES 59
Chapter 6 CHOOSING A TRANSFER FROM THE AIRPORT TO THE HOTEL AND BACK 66
Chapter 7 TRIP.COM – SEARCH ENGINE FOR TRIPS AND ATTRACTIONS NEARBY 69
Chapter 8 FLIGHT FROM BRATISLAVA TO DALAMAN, TURKEY 72
  Practical Traveller's Plan 85
  Packing Checklist 87
  (Verify before you leave) 87
  Conclusion 92
  About the Author 94

Prologue

Travel with Joy, Efficiency, and a Heart Full of Experiences

Imagine holding in your hands the key to new adventures that will brighten your days and fill your heart. That's exactly what this e-book offers – a guide for everyone who longs to travel more, smarter, more efficiently, and above all, with joy!

Travelling doesn't have to be just a dream anymore! You don't have to be a millionaire to explore the world – all it takes is a bit of enthusiasm, courage, and this book, which will show you how. Forget your worries about costs and start making your dreams of beautiful beaches, enchanting cities, and natural wonders come true.

Plan the vacation of your dreams – easily, affordably, and with a smile!

Let me welcome you to the doorstep of a new adventure. Imagine closing your eyes and feeling the scent of foreign lands in the air, the sea whispering around you, and unfamiliar alleys calling your steps. This guide wasn't written by chance – I wrote it with a heart wide open to every desire for discovery, relaxation, and the thrill that comes with the start of every journey.

I want your planning to become a pleasure, not just a task to check off. Listen to your inner visions: Will it be the roaring wind of adventure, the salty breeze on a coastline, or the whisper of culture hidden in the cobblestones of old towns? In any case, I've prepared a travel guide that will lead you step by step—from the initial idea through practical tips to the small details that turn a trip into an unforgettable experience.

I'm convinced that on the following pages, you'll discover not only new information but also inspiration you can use not only when planning a vacation but also in your everyday life and while browsing your favourite travel websites. Believe me, we all have a traveller inside us just waiting for the right moment to set out. So don't hesitate – let yourself be guided. This e-book is here for your determination, to turn beautiful dreams into reality.

Introduction

People travel for all sorts of reasons—some seek adventure, others crave peace, and some want to discover new cultures or meet new people. I travel because it brings me joy. I love that feeling when I sit down on a plane and the whole world lies before me like a blank book waiting to be written.

But I'll be honest—it wasn't always this way. I used to dream of travelling, but the fear of costs held me back. Package holidays through travel agencies felt like a luxury I couldn't afford. And when we tried to go on trips as a family, it usually ended up causing us financial stress.

That all changed when I discovered tips and tricks for travelling cheaper, smarter, and with more freedom. Today, I enjoy four holidays a year and always come home with a smile, well-rested and full of unforgettable memories.

If you long to experience the same joy of travelling, this book is just for you.

Inside, you'll find concrete tips, guides, trusted websites, and my personal recommendations to help you plan your adventures efficiently and effortlessl, without stress and with joy in your heart.

And the best part? You don't have to give anything up. Comfort, experiences, and savings can all go hand in hand beautifully. At the end of the book, you'll find a practical worksheet – fill it out, and turn your dream vacation into a solid plan.

Welcome, my dear travellers in spirit and soul!

I'm Anna, and I believe travel can brighten your thoughts, spark your imagination, and transform ordinary days into unforgettable experiences.
It is with great joy that I invite you on a special journey – not by plane to a distant country (though that will come too), but on a trip full of inspiration, ideas, and a little spark that awakens the desire to explore the world around us. I truly believe that dreams are meant to come true – and that travel doesn't have to be a luxury reserved only for the chosen few.

I'll Show You How to Travel Smartly, with a Smile, and Without Breaking the Bank

Yes, *you* can enjoy a holiday, a trip, or a quick escape from everyday life and gain amazing travel experiences—on your terms.

What Awaits You in This Book?

I've prepared practical and tried-and-tested tips for you, gathered from my journeys.
These suggestions will make planning easier, save you money and unnecessary worries, and—most importantly—bring you more joy from discovering the world!

Together, we'll look at:
✦ How to choose a destination that fits you perfectly,
✦ Where to find great deals on flights and accommodation,
✦ How to create a budget that doesn't limit you, but inspires you,
✦ and many other tricks I've tested myself—and they work!

So, what do you say? Will you join me?
I'm thrilled to accompany you on your journey toward your travel dreams!

With love, joy, and loads of energy,
Yours, Anna.

What Will You Learn? How to…

🌍 plan your holiday your way – calmly, efficiently, and stress-free,

✈ book flights through low-cost airlines without hidden fees,

🔍 find the best prices and reserve beautiful, affordable accommodation,

combine great flight and hotel deals,

🚐 arrange transfers from the airport straight to your dream hotel,

📍 discover interesting places and attractions nearby,

🏃 and use your savings to enjoy even more joy, relaxation, and unforgettable experiences.

All this – simply, with a smile, and a thirst for discovery.

Chapter 1

THE PLAN

How to Plan Ideally?

It's no secret that the best time to start planning next year's vacation is today—or ideally, right after returning from your last trip—when your memories are still fresh, your heart is full of excitement, and your head is brimming with new dreams. Planning your vacation well in advance is a crucial step toward ensuring a pleasant and stress-free travel experience.

Why Is It Worth Planning?

✺ ***Better Prices:*** Planning in advance gives you access to the best deals on flights, accommodation, or travel packages.

✺ ***More Options:*** Dates, destinations, types of hotels, and rooms are all open and available.

✺ ***Peaceful Planning:*** Without the rush and

stress, you can calmly prepare your budget, compare options, and avoid expensive last-minute solutions.

The best part about planning early is that the joy of travelling begins already in the preparation phase. You can take your time reading reviews, looking forward to the places you want to visit, creating your "must-see" lists, and daydreaming over a cup of coffee with a map in hand.

My Tip: Create a travel notebook or planning sheet where you jot down all your ideas, links, photos, and inspirations—you'll have everything in one place, and planning will become a fun new hobby.
You should ask yourself: *"Where do I feel drawn to the most?"* To the sea, the mountains, an adventurous road trip, or a relaxing city full of history? A vacation doesn't begin with the flight—it begins the moment you start dreaming about it.

With love and joy in planning,
Anna.

Together, We'll Explore

- How to define your vacation goals—whether you crave mountains, sea, adventure, or relaxation,

- How to choose the perfect destination based on your dreams.

- How to create a vacation plan—including the length of stay, excursions, and ideal timing,

- What to watch out for when considering season, weather, and prices. How to do a bit of research so you fall in love with your chosen destination even before you arrive.

❋ *Tips to Help You Out*

- Use Google Earth and Google Maps before your vacation to explore the beaches, the area around your hotel, and the overall destination.
- Keep track of and read hotel reviews – they can reveal a lot.
- Learn why it's a good idea to sign up for platforms like Booking.com, Agoda, or Trip.com – and how these accounts can make your travel easier.

Travel is about freedom, joy, experiences, and memories that no one can take away from you. I believe this book will be your companion on the journey to your dreams, helping you plan a holiday that reflects your heart's desires and lets you enjoy moments filled with energy, peace, and happiness.

I'm excited to meet you within the pages of this e-book and to see your traveller's soul shine bright.

Vacation Planning Can Be Fun

At first glance, it may seem like a lot of organising, but trust me, planning your dream vacation can be a beautiful and creative process. It's like piecing together a puzzle of joy, where every part leads to unforgettable experiences.

Here are a few key steps to successful #vacation_planning:

1. Define Your Goals

Ask yourself—what does your heart truly long for? Decide what you expect from your #vacation.

Do you want to lounge on a beach with a book in hand and the sound of the sea in the background? Or are you drawn to adventure, hiking, new flavours, culture, or adrenaline? Define your travel dreams, and everything will begin to fall into place. Understanding your goals will help you choose the right destination and plan your activities.

2. Choose a Destination

The —look at photos, reviews, and videos—and let yourself be swept away.
Every country has its unique charm, and somewhere out there is your dream destination. You can pick a place you've never been and consider various factors like culture, activities, natural beauty, adventure, or simple relaxation. If you're considering multiple destinations, do your research and compare their pros and cons before booking.

3. Create Your #Perfect_Vacation Plan

Grab a cup of coffee or your favourite drink, sit back, and start dreaming on paper.

Once you've chosen your destination, define the following:

✈ Where would you like to travel?

🛬 **Length of stay and the time of year** you'll visit the destination

📅 **Trips or excursions** you'd like to take during your stay

💰 **How much would you like (and be able) to spend?**

🌡 **What's the weather like** during the time you've chosen to visit? Look up air and sea temperatures, and check whether it's the rainy season, for instance.

What experiences do you want to have?

🌡 Also, check if the destination offers **pleasant temperatures even off-season**—prices will often be more budget-friendly.

Do a bit of research:

- Will the destination suit your preferences?
- Do you want to hike in the mountains?
- Relax on the beach?
- Engage in active rest?
- Or maybe you like a mix of both?

By now, your mind is likely drifting into daydreams, thinking about how to secure the right budget so you can travel without financial worries. But vacation planning isn't just about dates and prices.

It's about the *joy of anticipation*, about that butterfly feeling in your stomach when you imagine walking along a beach, tasting something delicious and unfamiliar, smiling at strangers who become part of your story...

To Kick Off Your Vacation Planning, Here Are a Few Quick Tips:

• *Set your goals and budget*

Your budget should be your best friend. You might be surprised how much beauty and joy you can experience even with a modest budget. Visualise where you'd love to go, how you want to feel there, and what you want to experience… Then align those goals with a realistic travel budget to help bring your dream to life.

• ***My Tip:*** Travelling outside of peak season not only saves you money but also lets you enjoy a more peaceful atmosphere.

• ***Start Saving Early*** – regularly or even irregularly, based on what's possible for you. Every euro brings you one step closer to your destination! It's amazing to watch how small amounts can turn into a big "wow."

• ***Avoid Debt And Travel With A Clear Mind***

Vacations should bring joy, not stress. That's why I strongly advise against taking loans for travel. Instead, break down your vacation costs into smaller steps and manageable payments. It's easier, more relaxed, and stress-free.

- Here's an example of how to break down a summer trip:
- Buy affordable flights in spring
- Soon after, book your accommodation with a small deposit—or even with payment upon arrival
- By summer, you'll have saved up for the rest of your lodging costs and some spending money, with funds left over for fun and excursions!
- Compare prices for the same accommodation on different travel sites and grab the best deal for the same hotel.

Small Travel Hacks That Really Pay Off

- Try saving at least €1000–2000 during winter – you'll be ready for early bookings when prices are at their best.
- On Booking.com, take advantage of the Genius loyalty program – 10–15–20% discounts are nothing to ignore.
- Agoda.com offers great combo deals when extending your stay.
- Stayforlong.com gives temporary discounts that last only a few hours – worth checking regularly!
- Don't forget about "My World Cash"—you collect cashback percentages from purchases, and from €10, you can transfer them back to your account. It's not a lottery win, but hey—every little bit counts.

Dear travelers, I'm saving the topic of accommodation as the cherry on top for later—and trust me, I've got some delicious travel tips in store that will not only save you money but also make your whole trip even more enjoyable!

So stay tuned and ride this positive wave with me—and don't forget: every day is the right day to start a new adventure!

Let's Start Planning Practically – With a Smile on Your Face and Excitement in Your Heart
How Many Days Do You Need to Truly Relax and Travel?

If you already know how many days you need to unwind, explore, and enjoy joyful moments just for yourself – that's fantastic news.

From my own experience, 7–8 days is just the warm-up into holiday mode. True relaxation usually begins

around day 10 or beyond. The first day is for settling in, the last for packing…
So give yourself the time to truly soak in the peace, sunshine, scents, and experiences – aim for *at least 10 days* to fully enjoy your getaway.

And now for a little challenge: your budget doesn't have to be a limitation. On the contrary – it's a wonderful opportunity to discover places that are not only charming but also affordable.

Keep in mind that some destinations are generally more expensive for travel and stays, while others can be much more budget-friendly. It's important to research in advance the local prices for food, accommodation, and services.

Another useful tip – many destinations offer their best outside of the peak season, surprising you not only with their beauty but also with lower prices.

Accommodation, good food, and getting around don't have to cost a fortune – in fact, with the right timing and a bit of clever planning, you can enjoy more experiences for less.
More flavors, more stunning spots, more laughter and joy… And below, I'll share more heartfelt tips to help shape your travel dreams, step by step.

We're Building Travel Dreams, One Step at a Time – Tips from the Heart:

• Big cities are usually more expensive, but quiet outskirts often hide true gems – lower prices, nature, calm, and a charm you'll fall in love with 💔

• Travelling by bus, train, rental car, or even on foot can be not only more budget-friendly but also part of the adventure 🚶‍♀️🚌
• If you're travelling with family, remember that your choice of accommodation, number of days, and meal plans (breakfast, half board, or full board) will affect your budget – but everything can be beautifully adjusted to suit your preferences ✿

2. Searching with a Smile – The Practical and Fun Way

And now comes the fun part. Open your browser and type Google.com into the address bar. In the search field, enter keywords and phrases—or if you already know them, type the names of places where you dream of spending your vacation, where your heart is pulling you 💙.

Let's search *practically and joyfully*:

For example, if you want to visit Turkey, try keywords like:
• *"Most beautiful beaches near Dalaman"*

Want to go to Mauritius?
Search something like:
• *"Most beautiful beaches in Mauritius"*
...and so on.

Let's take the example of:
"Most beautiful beaches near Dalaman"
Google immediately brings up a result in the first paragraph, with a link:

"The most beautiful beach is said to be the 3-kilometer-long beach in the resort of Ölüdeniz."

That's how I stumbled upon Ölüdeniz in my own search—a stunning piece of paradise near Fethiye in Muğla Province, Turkey—and just like that, I decided: *this is where I'm going—Ölüdeniz it is!*

You see, Google.com will often reveal amazing natural gems right in the first few lines of your search—places you may not have even heard of before.

The world is just a click away— you just need to know how to search smart.
Travel is joy and adventure, and when you plan from the heart, it can truly change your life.

The Right and Magical Keywords Can Open the Door to Discovery and Travel

Try searching with phrases like:

- *most beautiful beaches,*
- *most breathtaking mountain resorts,*
- *cities full of history,*
- *the most picturesque villages.*

Plan Your Trip with Heart, Mind – and a Smile!

When planning a vacation, countless beautiful details come into play—one of them being the number of people travelling. Naturally, the more people you travel with, the more thoughtful you'll need to be about dividing your budget wisely.
But that doesn't mean giving up a beautiful experience.

Sometimes, you'll choose fewer nights, simpler yet comfortable and affordable accommodation, or save on meals by opting for just breakfast or half-board. Even transportation can become part of the experience—a rental car, public transport, or romantic walks—each option has its own charm and might be just right for you.

Chapter 2

CHOOSING YOUR IDEAL DESTINATION

One crucial tip when selecting a destination is to check the weather patterns for the time of year you're planning to travel. Even the sun follows a calendar! ☀

That means before you settle on dates, always verify the climate in your chosen destination. It's easy—just go to one of the following sites to check air and sea temperatures, rainfall, or other weather conditions for your target period:

- weather.com
- accuweather.com
- meteo.com
- Or simply use Google

Checking these details will help ensure your trip aligns with the kind of experience you're dreaming of.

You'll find not only current forecasts but also long-term climate statistics, which will help you plan your vacation at the most beautiful time of year.

Just type into your search bar:
"Air and sea temperature in Ölüdeniz"

Weather sites are like little magic helpers—they tell you exactly *when and where* to go for the most pleasant vacation. With just a few clicks, you'll know the temperatures to expect, how warm the water is, and whether you should pack sunglasses or an umbrella.

Planning to visit Turkey in July? A quick glance at the forecast will tell you if it's the right time for you.

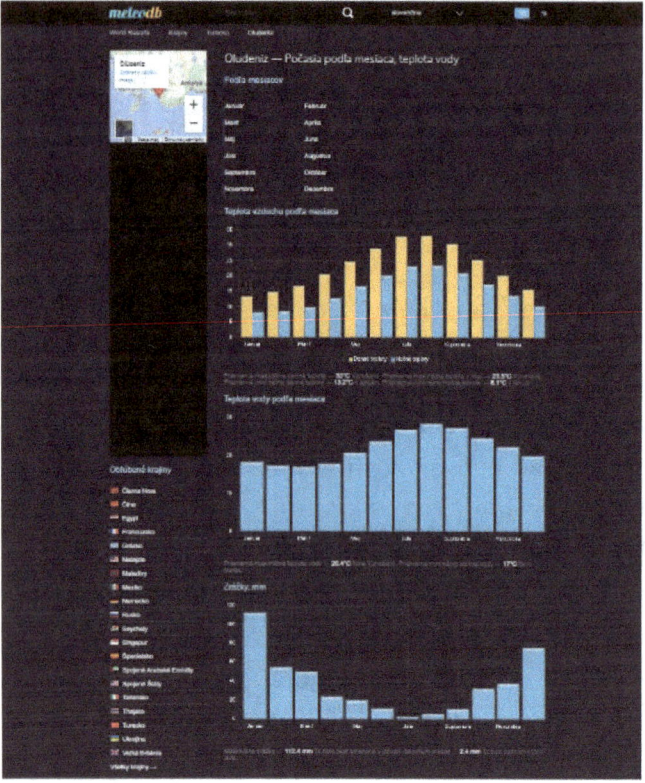

☞ Don't forget: every country has its own *"ideal season."*

While you can bask in the sun and enjoy tapas in Spain in the summer, Thailand might greet you with monsoon rains, and in the Seychelles, it might be peak rainy season. A well-timed holiday—weather-wise—means more adventure, fewer worries.

Chapter 3

FLIGHTS

Low-Cost Airlines

The next step is building a vacation plan that can save you a good amount of money.
Let's start with flights and explore a few options for buying them cheaper and smarter—without stress.

✈ *3.1 Flights – How to Buy Cheap, Smart, and Stress-Free*

Let's focus on low-cost airlines, which can make your travel dreams come true even on a smaller budget. There are many, but here are the ones I fly with the most. Of course, these tips and strategies can be applied to any of your favorite budget airlines.

3.1.a Ryanair

An Irish low-cost carrier and *queen of cheap flights in Europe.*
• Operates in over 40 countries
• Flies from Bratislava, London, Vienna, Budapest,

Kraków, and more
• Often uses secondary airports (e.g., Bergamo near Milan)

3.1.b EasyJet

A British airline with an extensive network across Europe and beyond.
• Focused on short- and mid-haul flights
• Flies to over 150 destinations in 35 countries

3.1.c Wizz Air

A Hungarian airline, especially popular for flights from Budapest, Vienna, and Košice.
• Great for weekend getaways and seaside vacations
• Affordable, comfortable, and offers frequent connections

Low-Cost Airlines – Ryanair

Ryanair is a low-cost airline that allows you to travel affordably across Europe. For example, you can fly from Bratislava Airport to several destinations in Europe, and from Vienna Airport, you can reach even more countries (as shown in the referenced image).

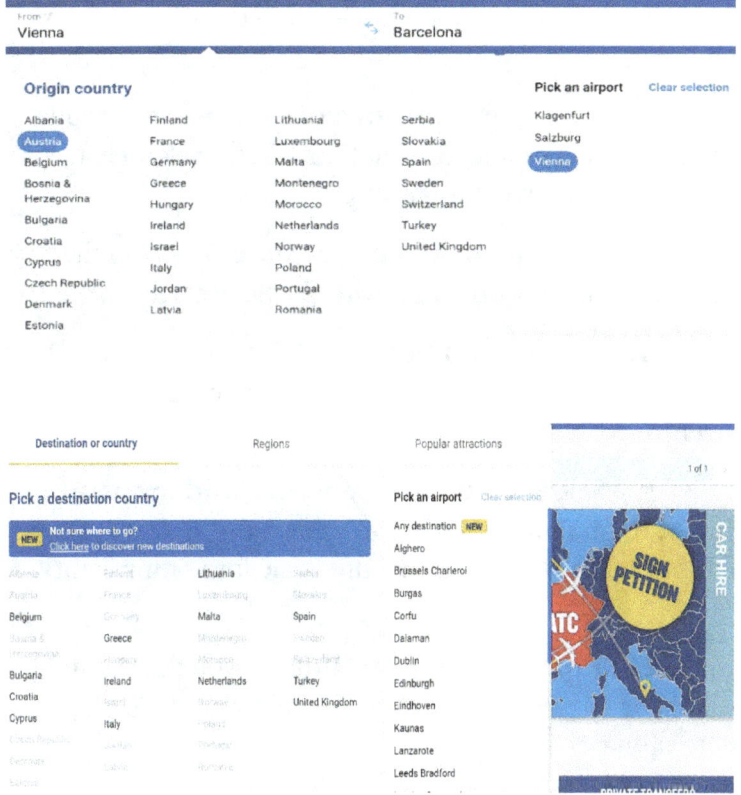

How to Avoid Unnecessary Fees When Booking Flights?

Want to travel smart and save money for experiences instead of extra charges? Here's a simple and joyful step-by-step guide to booking a cheap flight with Ryanair—stress-free and with a smile:

✅ **1. Log in to your Ryanair account** at ryanair.com – the login is in the top right corner. If you don't have an account yet, create one – it only takes a few minutes.

✓ **2. Search for your dream route** – enter your departure location and destination. Click on Search and explore the options Ryanair offers!

✓ **3. Select your departure date** –click on the day that suits you and confirm it with the Select button.

✓ **4. Choose your return flight** the same way. For example: *Bratislava – Dalaman*. And your summer adventure can begin!

✓ **5. Pick your ideal departure and arrival times.** Several options will be displayed—choose the one that fits you best. Then select the Basic fare – this is the cheapest option.

✓ **6. Skip the seat selection** – if you don't mind where you sit, choose Continue without a seat. You'll save more money!

✓ **7. Baggage?** If you're traveling light, one small personal item (40x20x25 cm) is included for free.

✓ **8. Enter your personal details** and document number (passport or ID – depending on your destination).

✓ **9. Avoid adding extras** like insurance, car rental, or bus transfer unless you truly need them.

✓ **10. Click Continue**, enter your payment details, and... done! Your tickets are booked. 🎉

Travelling on a budget doesn't mean compromising joy. Plan smart, book cleverly, and keep more for the things that matter—experiences, flavours, and stories to tell.

Baggage & Check-In: Travel Smart, Save More

Make sure to check in online from home – it's a simple move that saves you from unnecessary airport fees.

✈ Smart Check-In Tips:

- Print your boarding pass or save it to your mobile phone
- Printing at the airport may cost you extra – avoid those fees!
- Select your baggage type at the time of ticket purchase – adding it later at the airport is significantly more expensive
- Double-check baggage dimensions before your flight – if your luggage is too big, you could be fined

Ryanair Grace Period – A Helpful Freebie

Within 24 hours of booking, you can change the name or flight date for free, but:

- ✓ This only applies if you booked through the Ryanair app or official website

- ✗ It does not apply if you booked through third-party sites (like Pelikán, Kiwi)

Top Tip: Search Smart, Buy Smart

- Use flight comparison tools like Skyscanner, Azair, or Pelikán to search for deals
- But book directly through the portal offering the lowest price

WIZZ Discount Club Light – No Membership Fee!

If you're flying with Wizz Air and want to enjoy a nice snack on board while saving a few euros on souvenirs, this one's for you.

WIZZ Discount Club Light is perfect for occasional travelers who like perks without long-term commitments.

Benefits include:

✓ Discounts on in-flight meals
✓ Better prices on onboard boutique items
✓ Simple activation via the Wizz Air app

Travel doesn't have to be expensive—just smart.

Standard WIZZ Discount Club – For True Travellers

Do you dream of bigger discounts and comfort all year round? Then the WIZZ Discount Club is made for you! For a small annual fee, you'll gain access to year-round travel benefits that will delight both your wallet and your wanderlust.

✈ Perks include:

• Discounts on all flights, all year long
• Coupons for onboard boutique shopping
• Special offers for in-flight meals

So, are you ready to join a club where travel is smart and joyful?
Flying with Wizz Air is not only budget-friendly—it frees up money for even more adventures.

3.2 Pelikan.sk – Your Gateway to Affordable Adventures

Travel isn't just about destinations—it's a mindset. Sometimes the urge to go somewhere strikes *before* you've even checked your bank account. But that doesn't have to stop you anymore.

Pelikan.sk, a trusted Slovak travel portal since 2004, offers airfares that will pleasantly surprise you—often cheaper than expected. Thanks to smart features, you'll never miss a great deal again.

💡 *Smart Traveller Tip*

Sign up, create an account, and activate flight deal alerts.
Best part? These deal gems land in your inbox three hours

before they go live on the website. That edge can mean the difference between flying for €40 or €140!

Pro Tip from Me:
Download the Pelikan app to your phone and always be ready to grab a sweet deal to Paris, Tokyo, or Caribbean beaches.

Timing Is Everything with Promotions

The best deals sell out in just a few hours. So if you've found your dream destination, book quickly and without hesitation. This rule applies to nearly all airlines and ticket sellers.

Booking Strategy:

• For European destinations, book flights 4–6 weeks in advance.
• For long-haul exotic destinations, track prices months ahead—even up to 6 months. The price difference can be €500–€1500, and that's well worth the effort.

With low-cost flights from Vienna, Budapest, Bratislava, Kraków, and other Central European cities, your dream trip is within reach—even if you don't live near the coast.

Once your ticket is booked, don't forget to look for accommodation right away.
Through Pelikan, you can easily find a hotel that fits your taste and take care of everything with just a few clicks.

3.3 EasyJet – British Classic Among Low-Cost Airlines

If you crave spontaneous trips to London, Edinburgh, or sunny Andalusia, easyJet is your ideal ticket to a world of adventure without having to dip into your savings.

This British low-cost airline flies to over 150 destinations and offers transparent prices that often pleasantly surprise you.

Tip for smart travelers:

✓ Watch for deals on the official website easyjet.com

✓ Subscribe to the newsletter to gain access to special offers

✓ Travel with carry-on luggage only – save money and be faster than others!

If you love efficiency, punctuality, and airports like London Gatwick or Manchester, easyJet is your orange runway to travel.

3.4 British Airways – Elegantly and Comfortably Around the World

If you enjoy travelling in the style of "British nobility" at a reasonable price, then you should consider tickets with British Airways, the United Kingdom's national airline with a long-standing tradition, which is the ideal choice for:

✓ Long-haul flights to America, the Caribbean, Asia

✓ Comfortable connections from London (especially from Heathrow)

✓ Travellers who want a higher standard without unnecessary fees.

Travel tip:

Watch for "Flight + Hotel" deals directly on britishairways.com, where you can often find discounted packages that also include hotels at a good price. If you like loyalty programs, the Executive Club program allows you to collect Avios points and fly even more advantageously.

3.5 Search Engines for Flight and Accommodation Booking

1. **Google**
   You can find flights using Google's very fast and user-friendly tool (Google Flights) at flights.google.com. It shows prices from various portals and price trends over time.

2. **Skyscanner** skyscanner.net
   This is an excellent portal for comparing prices from different carriers and travel agencies. It allows searching by the cheapest months.

3. **Kayak** kayak.com
   Very good for flight combinations, especially with multiple destinations. It also shows alternative airports.

4. **Pelikan.sk** pelikan.sk
   A Slovak portal with Slovak language support, where you can find interesting deals and learn about combining flight + hotel options.

5. **Kiwi.com** kiwi.com
   This portal is suitable for finding less traditional routes and combined connections, often with transfers by different carriers.

6. **Cheapflights.co.uk**
   A specialist in deals and advantageous offers, especially from London and Manchester.

Accommodation Search Engines

7. **Booking.com** booking.com
   The largest accommodation portal – from hotels through apartments to guesthouses. Offers filtering by ratings, price, and location.

8. **Airbnb** airbnb.com
   Offers a great selection of private accommodation

and local experiences. An ideal portal for an authentic experience.

9. **Agoda** agoda.com
A strong player especially for Asia, but with a growing offer in Europe as well. You will find good prices and various discounts.

10. **Trivago** trivago.com
Compares hotel prices from different portals and recommends where a particular hotel is cheapest.

11. **Hotels.com** hotels.com
A portal that offers a loyalty program – every 11th night is free. Often publishes advantageous last-minute deals.

12. **Expedia.co.uk** expedia.co.uk
Combines flights + hotels at a discounted price. Suitable for complete packages (e.g., city breaks).

13. **Lastminute.com UK** lastminute.com
It's perfect for last-minute weekend stays, luxury packages, or flights and hotels together. It also has a "Top Secret Hotels" section with reduced prices.

Other well-known search engines include:
14. Momondo.com
15. Opodo.com
16. Reserving.com

Reserving.com is an online booking portal based in Spain, offering:

✓ Hotels, apartments, guesthouses, villas

✓ Tailor-made holidays (hotel + tickets packages, hotel + wellness, etc.)

✓ Advantageous offers for families, groups, or romantic stays

Why consider it:
• Payment in instalments without interest – if you book well in advance, you can pay in several smaller instalments
• Numerous offers in Spain, Italy, Greece, and across Europe
• Price guarantee – if you find a cheaper price elsewhere, they will refund the difference
• Great customer service in English and Spanish

Use for UK:
✓ Available in English (including offers from London, Manchester, etc.)
✓ Option to filter accommodation by location, price, type, or rating
✓ Suitable also for families travelling from the UK to summer destinations

3.5.2 I Have a Destination Selected

Momondo.com is also an excellent portal for searching flights. Momondo is a Danish search engine for flights, hotels, and car rentals that compares prices from dozens of different websites, including airlines, travel agencies, and other comparison sites.

Advantages:
✓ Very clear and colourful interface
✓ Shows the cheapest, fastest, and best value options
✓ Price graph over time – easily see when flights are cheapest
✓ Filters by price, flight duration, airports, layovers, etc.
✓ No hidden fees – shows final prices
✓ Also has a mobile app

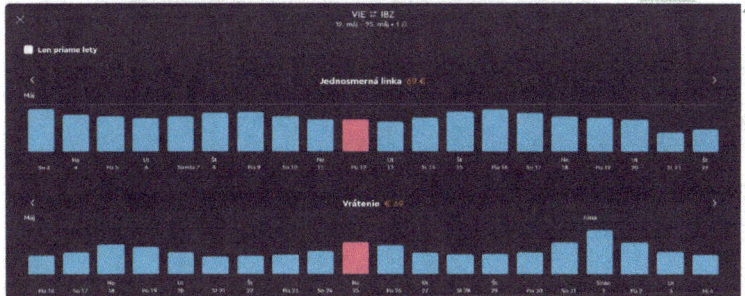

I Don't Have a Destination Selected

Choose your travel destination through Momondo or Skyscanner based on the best flight price. If you are still unsure where to direct your travel steps, and at the same time, you want the best flight price, here's a simple trick to discover fascinating offers that will open new horizons for you. Travelling is all about adventure and discovering unknown places, and sometimes the most beautiful adventure comes when you let yourself be carried away by price offers that can change your whole perspective on the world.

Simply use some flight search engines like Momondo or Skyscanner, etc., where you can enter just the best date and preferences for price range, and discover destinations that fit your budget. You might find a place you never dreamed of, but that's where your new travel adventure hides.

Make the price your ticket to a world full of new experiences that you can enjoy whether you already had a destination on your list or decided based solely on the available price offer. Travelling is most beautiful when you allow yourself to be surprised by the local beauty and enchanting culture.

How to Use momondo.com

If you don't yet have a destination selected, here is a simple method to find and visit interesting destinations by using the best flight prices:

1. Enter your departure location and travel date in the search engine (e.g., Momondo or Skyscanner).

2. On search engines like Momondo or Skyscanner, you can easily choose flights to destinations using an interactive map.

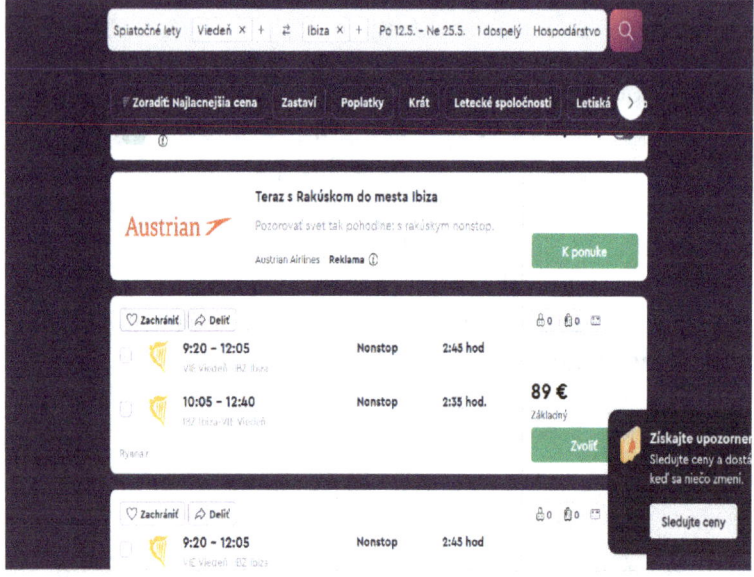

3. Here's how to do it:
   Type in your departure place and travel date. Leave the arrival place blank and click the small blue magnifying glass on the right side. Then click on "Explore." Move the screen using the technique "hold the left mouse button, drag, and release." This way, you can move the entire map and navigate to destinations that interest you.

You didn't select an airport

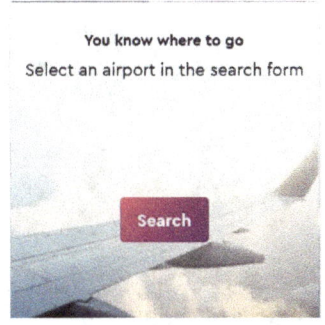
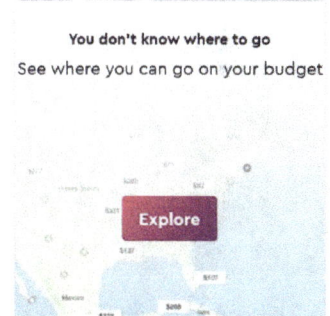

4. Hover your mouse over a spot on the map representing your chosen destination. At that moment, flight prices will appear from the airport you initially entered, for example, from Vienna to the selected locations.

5. Besides flights, you can also choose combinations of flight + hotel or use other special offers, including discounts on flights, hotels, and stays. After selecting a destination, click on the country to see more special offers and advantageous prices. Then all that's left is to book your flight.

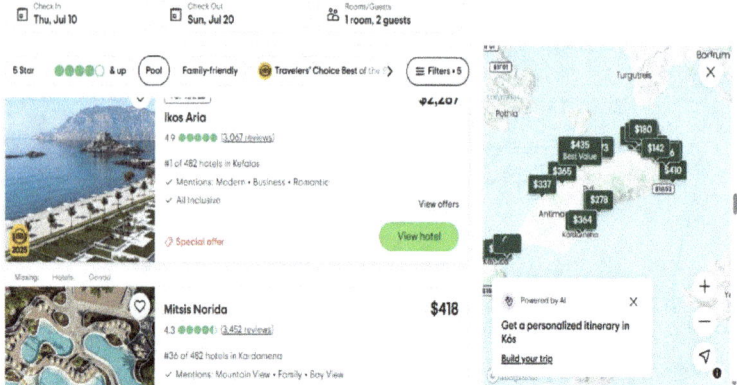

Although this is a simple and advantageous way to find cheap flights, it is important to be aware that claims or changes can be difficult to make on Momondo, Opodo, Skyscanner, since they act as sales intermediaries.

Discover the World with Opodo.com

Opodo is a British online portal offering flights, hotels, car rentals, and holiday packages. It belongs to the eDreams ODIGEO group and has a strong presence, especially in Europe. This web portal is like a gateway to a world of endless travel possibilities—whether you're looking for flights, hotels, or a complete tailor-made stay.

Advantages:

✅ Opodo Prime membership – significant discounts on flights and hotels throughout the year

✅ Often find prices lower than on official airline websites

✅ Option to buy a complete package (flight + hotel) at a better price

✅ Mobile app with easy reservation management

💡 **Note:** If you travel more than once a year, Opodo Prime is worth it, as your investment often pays off with the first trip.

On Opodo.com, you can choose exactly what suits you best—from a standalone flight, accommodation, to advantageous flight + hotel packages. Just click on the "More" option in the main menu, and a world of destinations will open before you, instantly pulling you in. With one click, you'll get to the place you've always dreamed of.

Simple Search with the Explore Button

Once you confirm your choice, just click the prominent red "Explore" button. This will direct you to an overview of price offers per person for the selected destination. Everything is clear, fast, and ready, so you can set off on your adventure without lengthy deliberation.

Attractive Offers for Trips and Experiences

Click, for example, on California—and a complete offer of current flight prices, comfortable hotels, and tours will open before you, all bookable in just a few clicks. Whether you long for adventures in national parks, walks on beaches, or the bustling life of big cities, Opodo.com will help you plan a trip you'll remember for a long time.

Lastminute.com

Lastminute.com (or Lastminute.de) is a popular portal for finding flights and accommodation. I have often booked flights and hotels through this site and have always been pleasantly surprised. Besides great prices, the portal also offers free online check-in, and your ticket is sent directly to your email, which greatly simplifies the process.

Why You'll Love Lastminute.com

If you're like me, you want to enjoy your holiday without stress—and save money at the same time. That's exactly why I discovered Lastminute.com—a site where everything operates quickly, simply, and to your advantage.

Save More Than You Expect

When you choose a flight + hotel package on Lastminute.com, you save a significant amount of money. The package costs less than if you bought everything separately. And you can spend those savings on something much nicer—like a great dinner with a sea view.

You Have a Handy Helper by Your Side

Lastminute.com finds the best combinations of flights and hotels for you. It monitors prices, flight duration, and departure times so you can make the most of your holiday. When it comes to hotels, it relies on reviews from people who have already stayed there—just like I would.

Booking That Takes Just a Moment

Instead of spending hours online, you can arrange everything in a few seconds. A few clicks and it's done. No stress, no unnecessary hesitation.

A Holiday According to Your Wishes

Want to fly with a specific airline and stay in a beautiful villa or modern apartment? On Lastminute.com, you can customize your package exactly how you feel—offering over 400 airlines and millions of accommodation options worldwide.

A Search That Really Listens to You

Even if you have specific preferences (for example, a hotel steps from the beach or an early morning flight to make the most of the day), Lastminute.com makes it easier for you. Just a few filters—and you find exactly what you're looking for.

Booking Option with a Small Deposit

If you already know where you want to travel in the summer months or at Christmas, take advantage of the Flight + Hotel option. This package allows you to book your holiday with a small deposit, while you can pay the rest later in small instalments, or even just before departure, with no hidden costs or interest.

Benefits of this Option:
• Flexibility in payment: The deposit is low and lets you spread payments into smaller amounts, making financial planning easier.
• No hidden costs: Prices are transparent, and you won't have to pay any hidden fees or interest.

Greater Protection When Booking
When you book a flight + hotel package, you get greater protection in case of unexpected changes. This package is protected under Directive No. 2302 of 2015, which means:
• Guaranteed protection: If the service provider cancels your flight or hotel, you are entitled to an alternative solution or the possibility to request a refund. This way, you have more confidence that your holiday will go smoothly even in unforeseen circumstances.

Search Options on Lastminute.com

1. **Flight Search**
   • When searching for flights, you can choose from various criteria:
   o **Best price:** If your goal is to find the cheapest flight.
   o **Fastest flight:** If you prefer the quickest flight, regardless of the price.
   o **Lowest price:** You can decide on the lowest price regardless of the trip duration.

2. **Hotel Prices on the Map**
   • The hotel price map is very useful because when you click on a price on the map, a specific hotel matching that price offer will appear. This allows

you to quickly see options in particular areas and find the best deals within your requirements.

3. **Holiday Search by Criteria**

- **Location:** Enter a place, such as a specific sea, city, or country you want to visit.
- **Multiple Dates:** You can specify the number of nights and then select the "Any date" option. This allows you to choose flexible dates and compare offers over several months.
- **Anywhere:** If you are flexible and open to new destinations, choose your preferred holiday period and compare the best deals worldwide. This approach helps you discover interesting places and offers based on your available time.

This approach enables you to get advantageous offers according to different preferences while ensuring flexibility in holiday planning.

Search Options on Kiwi.com

Kiwi offers truly flexible options when searching for flights, especially if you have time flexibility and are willing to accept more extended layovers or waits between flights. Here are some key benefits and features Kiwi provides:

Advantages of Kiwi.com

1. **Cheap flights for longer journeys:** Kiwi can find very advantageous flight prices even if you have multiple layovers. This can be ideal if you don't mind spending more time at the airport and want to save money.

2. **Date flexibility:** If you leave your dates open, Kiwi will show flight prices for different days. This is very helpful if you want to find the cheapest option over several days in a given period.

3. **Price table:** After entering your departure and arrival locations, you can enable a price table that shows various flight prices on specific days. This is great if you have flexibility about when to fly and want to find the best price.

4. **Hotel prices on the map:** If you are also planning accommodation, the hotel price map is very practical. Just click on a price and the hotel with that price offer will appear, allowing you to see not only flights but also accommodation prices in the area.

- **Flight search:** Kiwi lets you choose between:
  - **Best price:** If your main focus is price and you are flexible.
  - **Lowest price:** For those who want to minimize flight costs.
  - **Fastest route:** If you prefer comfort and speed regardless of price.

Which option to choose?
• If you have flexibility in dates and prefer saving money, choosing the cheapest flight or best price might be most advantageous.
• If speed and comfort matter more to you (and you don't mind a higher price), choose the fastest flight option.

Depending on your priorities, you can pick the option that suits you best!

3. Advantages of Searching for Flights via Google

How to easily find the best flight deals?

If you try searching through Google, you will discover not only immediate flight prices but also prices for nearby dates.

If you feel like hitting the road and want to quickly and clearly map out what flights are available in the airline world, searching for flights through Google is truly a great choice. It's a simple way to have all options within reach—without having to browse through dozens of websites.

Quick price overview all in one place

Google displays prices from various airlines in a neat column chart. With just one glance, you can immediately see which offer is the most advantageous for you. This easy comparison allows you to choose a flight that will delight not only your traveler's heart but also offer lower costs.

Search that takes no more than a few minutes

Searching via Google is straightforward. You only need to enter three details: departure place, arrival place, and date. Google instantly loads a list of available flights, saving you long hours of searching and comparing.

You can book your flight immediately

When a deal catches your eye, just click—and Google will redirect you straight to the airline's or travel agency's website. Your flight ticket will be yours in just a few minutes, without unnecessary intermediaries or complicated procedures.

A handy graph shows the best days to travel

Another great tool is the price graph by date. Thanks to it, you can easily pick the day when flights are cheapest.

Sometimes just a small change in day or date can bring you big savings.

A little tip at the end

To get the best flight prices, watch offers ideally 4 to 6 weeks before your planned departure. The closer to the departure, prices generally tend to be higher. And don't forget to also check low-cost airlines' websites, like Ryanair or Wizz Air—real treasures sometimes hide there.

Thus, Google offers a fast, clear, and very effective way to secure the right flight—exactly according to your preferences.

Skyscanner.net – Your Smart Travel Companion

If you love to travel and want to save money on your trips, Skyscanner.net should definitely be part of your travel toolkit. This search engine has won the hearts of millions of travellers worldwide—and it's no surprise. It helps you quickly and easily compare prices for flights, hotels, and car rentals all in one place. What does Skyscanner offer you, and why will you love it?

1. All prices in one place

Skyscanner searches hundreds of airlines, hotels, and car rental companies to bring you the best options. This way, you don't have to waste hours clicking through dozens of websites—it's all neatly gathered for you.

2. Price change alerts

If you find a deal you like but aren't ready to decide yet, set up an alert. Skyscanner will email you as soon as the price changes. This way, you're sure not to miss the best time to buy.

3. Flexible searching

Unsure of your exact departure date? No worries!

Skyscanner displays prices for an entire month or even a whole year. Just select when the ticket is at its lowest price.

4. Discovering New Places

If you crave adventure and do not wish to be confined to a single destination, try the "Everywhere" feature. Enter your departure location, and Skyscanner will reveal the most affordable destinations around the globe. You may find yourself heading to a place you never imagined!

5. Handy mobile app

Whether you're sitting in a café or waiting for the bus, you can search for flights, hotels, and cars anytime and anywhere with the Skyscanner app.

How to Use Skyscanner for Different Purposes

- **Searching for flights:** Just enter your departure place, arrival place, and date—or use the "Cheapest month" option to find the best date.

- **Price alerts:** Track your selected favorite flights and get notified by email whenever the price changes.
- **Discovering new destinations:** If you're open to different options, the "Everywhere" feature shows you the most attractive destinations at great prices.

Tips to Get the Most Out of Skyscanner

If you're planning a vacation and want to save time and money, Skyscanner is a great help. Here's how to use it effectively:

1. Find the cheapest day to fly
Not sure exactly when you want to fly? No worries. On Skyscanner, when selecting the date, click on "Whole month." You'll see an overview of all days in that month and immediately know which days are cheapest. Pick one and fly for a fraction of the price!

2. Track flight price changes
If you've already chosen your destination and date but hesitate to book, set a price alert. Skyscanner will email you whenever the price changes, up or down. This way, you can wait for the best deal and buy your ticket at exactly the right time.

3. Find the best hotel prices
Skyscanner isn't just about flights! It also compares hotel prices from big players like Booking.com, Hotels.com, or Expedia. Using filters, you can easily set your preferred rating, price range, and how far from the city centre you

want to stay. Then pick accommodation exactly to your liking.

4. Watch hotel price changes too

Just like flights, you can turn on price alerts for hotels in Skyscanner. If accommodation gets cheaper or more expensive, Skyscanner will notify you by email. Thanks to that, you can secure a great place at a great price. Skyscanner is a comprehensive tool that can save you both time and money when planning your trips.

Chapter 4

ACCOMMODATION – BOOKING A STAY THAT WILL THRILL YOU!

How to Save When Booking Hotels: Little Secrets for Big Trips: Travelling is like a magical dance — sometimes it's a bold step into the unknown, other times a gentle twirl around the details that make a vacation unforgettable. And when it comes to booking a hotel, there are many smart decisions you can make that will save you money and make your stay more enjoyable.

1. Think Ahead

If you know when and where you want to travel, book your accommodation as early as possible. Early bookings often bring the lowest prices and a wider choice.

But beware, if you have an adventurous spirit and like to take risks, last-minute deals can sometimes surprise you with incredible discounts.

2. Compare, Compare, Compare

Check all available booking portals, such as Booking.com, Agoda, Hotels.com, Trip.com, and others. Each portal has its own prices, offers, and benefits. Sometimes, it pays to check the hotel's website, where special deals or better cancellation policies can be found.

3. Be Flexible

If you can slightly adjust your dates or pick a less busy period, your savings will thank you. Outside the high season, hotels are often half the price, and you'll enjoy more peace, sunshine, and local flavours without the crowds.

4. Use Loyalty Programs And Cashback

Many portals offer discounts for regular customers or cashback programs where part of your money is returned to your account. Little savings here and there can add up to more travel adventures later.

5. Watch For Special Offers And Codes

Some hotels and booking sites publish discount codes that bring extra perks—price reductions, free breakfast, or room upgrades. Just subscribe to their newsletters or follow them on social media.

6. Consider What You Really Need

Sometimes it's cheaper to book a hotel without breakfast and enjoy your morning coffee and croissant in a cosy local café. Or pick a hotel a few blocks from the centre, exchanging a higher price for peace, authenticity, and better value.

If you've already chosen your destination and bought or reserved your flights, it's time to find accommodation.

The most popular booking portals are:

- Booking.com
- Agoda.com
- Hotels.com
- Reserving.com
- Stayforlong.com
- MyLastminute.com
- MyLastminute.de
- ZenHotels.com
  ...and others.

Some of these portals also appeared in flight booking sections since they offer not only flights but also hotel reservations, taxi rentals, car hire, and more.

Today, you don't search for accommodation blindly—you have smart online portals and comparison sites that show you different prices for the same room in the same hotel. Believe me, the price differences can be surprisingly big.

Early booking is like a secret key to a carefree vacation, especially if you're travelling during the season to a popular destination. It lets you choose from the best hotels, boutique apartments, or romantic guesthouses exactly to your style and wishes.

You'll often find better prices, complimentary services, or favorable conditions that might otherwise slip away. That way, your trip will be pleasant from the start, because you'll know that at the end of the day, a cosy place is waiting for you to relax and recharge.

Booking.com

One of the most popular platforms for booking accommodation is Booking.com. It's a good idea to create an account and book directly through the site so you can accumulate discounts. By regularly booking accommodation via Booking.com, you can earn discounts of 5%, 10%, 15%, and even up to 20% off your stay — savings that stay with you forever. Additionally, you become a member of the Genius program, which offers discounts worth tens of euros on selected stays.

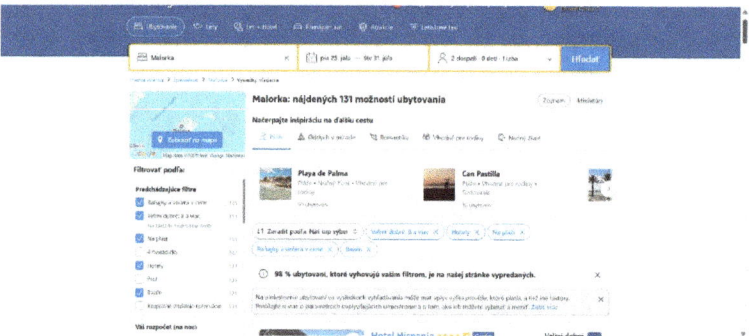

Before finalising your booking, don't forget to check the hotel on Google Maps. It's always wise to verify the surroundings to make sure there's no ongoing construction or noisy developments nearby that could disturb your peace and relaxation during your vacation.

Booking.com offers a variety of filters to help you find the perfect stay. You can select meal options such as no meals, breakfast only, half board, full board, or all-inclusive. You can also filter by accommodation type: hotel, apartment, hostel, holiday villa, and more. There are options tailored for adults, families with children, hotels with fitness centres, wellness and spa services, bike rentals, and much more.

An important step is to read guest reviews and ratings related to hotel services, quality of food and accommodation, distance from the beach, staff behaviour, cleanliness, proximity to the city centre or sea, and so on. These reviews reveal what other travellers think about the hotel's quality, comfort, and overall experience, helping you feel confident that your accommodation will truly meet your expectations.

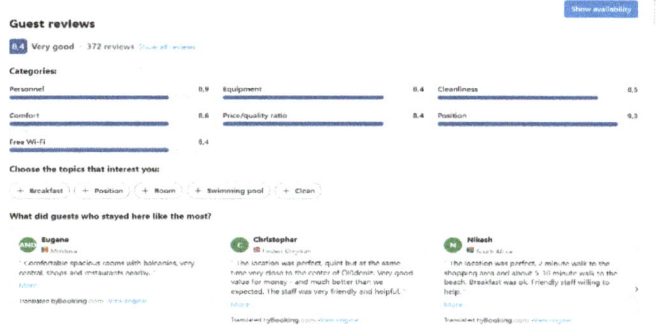

Choose Your Stay According to Your Preferences

Don't hesitate to create the vacation you've always dreamed of. Pick a place that will be your perfect paradise, and book a stay that fully satisfies you, whether it's a luxurious hotel or a cosy apartment. Great options await you at every turn.

Chapter 5

COMPARING ACCOMMODATION PRICES

5.1 Tripadvisor.com – A Comparer That Makes Your Travel Easier

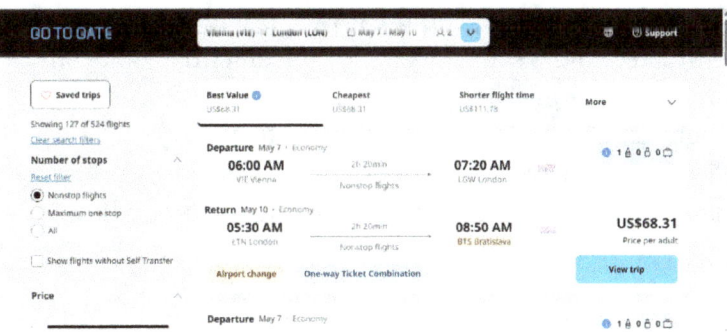

Tripadvisor.com is a search and comparison portal for flights as well as accommodation. Tripadvisor cooperates with flight providers such as Go to Gate, My Trip, eDreams,

Kiwi, Opodo, Ryanair, Vayama, Lastminute, Bravofly, Gate1, Kupi, and others.

Some links will take you directly to airline websites like Ryanair, and occasionally you may find lower flight prices through portals like Go to Gate.

Accommodation Through Tripadvisor – A Smart Price Comparer

When it comes to finding great accommodation, Tripadvisor is your ally. It cooperates with well-known platforms like Booking, Hotels.com, Expedia, Agoda, and many others, comparing prices for the same hotels from different sellers. This means you can quickly compare which seller offers the best price for the same accommodation and choose the best deal.

For example, if you look at the 3BQ Augusta Hotel, the price might be 171 EUR on Booking, but only 154 EUR on Stayforlong. Just click on the lowest price, and you will be redirected to the seller's page to conveniently book your accommodation. This way, you save both time and money when searching for the perfect place to stay.
Tip: To get the very best prices, use Tripadvisor to compare offers and choose the one that suits you best.

5.2 Trivago – Your Next Helper in Finding the Best Accommodation Prices

Trivago is a popular online search engine specializing in comparing accommodation prices for hotels, hostels, apartments, B&Bs, and other types of lodging. If you are planning a trip and looking for the ideal place to stay, Trivago provides all the necessary information in one place.

How Does It Work?

Trivago compares prices from over 700,000 hotels on more than 200 booking websites like Booking.com, Expedia, Priceline, and others. This means you get a wide range of accommodation options from all available sites.

Why Use Trivago?

- **Wide selection:** Whether you're looking for a luxury hotel, an affordable hostel, or an apartment — Trivago shows you all options across different price categories.
- **Time-saving:** No need to browse hundreds of different websites, Trivago does it for you. You save time and find the best deals.
- **Clarity:** The website is user-friendly, allowing you to easily compare prices and decide where to book your stay.

Tip: If you're planning your next vacation or business trip, don't forget to use Trivago. This portal will help you find accommodation that is not only comfortable but also cost-effective!

Accommodation Through Tripadvisor – Get The Best Price For Your Stay

Tripadvisor is another reliable helper when choosing accommodation. It is an excellent comparison portal that cooperates with various renowned companies, such as Booking.com, Trip.com, Hotels.com, Hyatt.com, Expedia.com, Agoda.com, Stayforlong.com, ZenHotels.com, Intercontinental.com, and many others, in numerous countries worldwide.

Why Use Tripadvisor?

1. ***Price Comparison:*** Tripadvisor compares accommodation prices per person/per night from multiple booking sites, offering you the best and most advantageous options for your stay.

2. ***Prices for The Same Accommodation:*** For example, if you choose the hotel "3BQ Augusta Hotel," it might cost 171 EUR on Booking.com, while on Stayforlong.com the price is only 154 EUR. This way, you can easily compare and decide on the best offer.

3. ***Quick and Convenient Decision-Making:*** Just click on the lowest price, and you will be redirected to the seller's page where you can easily complete your booking. It is a fast and efficient way to get the best deal on the market.

Advantages of Tripadvisor

Tripadvisor is an ideal tool for saving time and money when searching for accommodation. The portal compares prices from various providers and sellers. You might find different prices for the same hotel room. Tripadvisor allows you to see which site offers the best price for the same room in a given hotel, helping you make a smart, wise decision when booking. I therefore recommend using Tripadvisor.

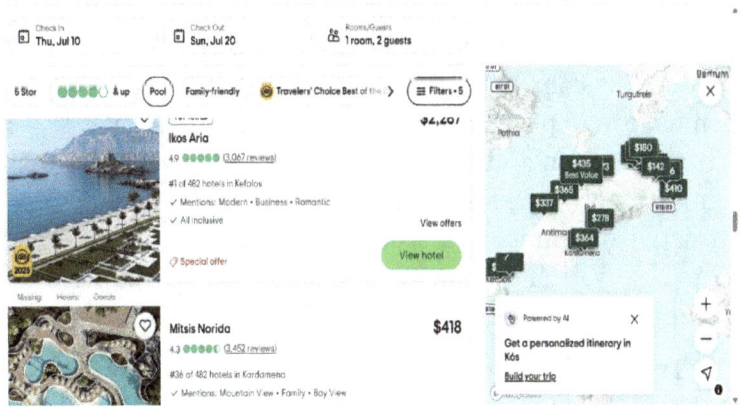

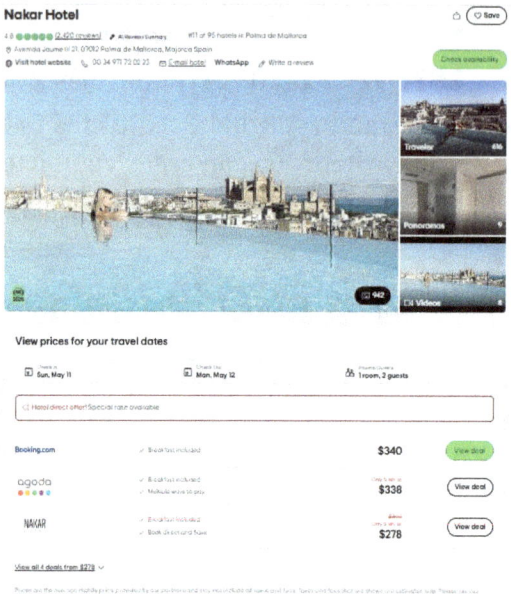

Advantages of Booking.com and Tripadvisor when booking accommodation and flights

Genius Program on Booking.com

On Booking.com, you can get special benefits through the Genius loyalty program, which offers discounts on accommodation and access to various exclusive deals. Just sign up and by making regular bookings, you can enjoy attractive discounts that accumulate with every stay. The more reservations you make, the bigger the discounts you can get — and it's definitely worth it.

Tripadvisor – Compare prices per night

On Tripadvisor.com, you can quickly compare prices for the same hotel from different sellers. By applying filters with specific conditions like dates, number of nights, accommodation type, etc., you get a selection of the best offers. Based on the price comparison, you choose the most advantageous offer that suits you. Then simply click on the lowest price and your booking is done.

Reviews – The key to choosing the right hotel

When choosing a hotel, reviews from previous guests are very important. Personally, I prefer accommodation in destinations with hotels rated "very good," meaning 8 or above. From traveller and guest reviews and experiences, you learn what to expect from the hotel, whether positive or negative aspects. A hotel with a rating of 8 or higher is generally a very good choice. Read as many reviews as possible beforehand to make sure your choice is the right one.

Google Maps and Google Earth – Test the hotel and its surroundings

For even more information, check out the hotel and its surroundings via Google Maps or Google Earth. These tools will show you whether the hotel actually exists, what the neighbourhood and beach look like. You can verify if the hotel is easily accessible and whether there is any construction noise or mess nearby. This information will help you make an informed decision about your stay.

Chapter 6

CHOOSING A TRANSFER FROM THE AIRPORT TO THE HOTEL AND BACK

Google is a great helper. Just type the right keywords into the search engine, and the solution will magically appear before you. Sometimes it's useful to tweak the keywords, as the website's search engine may find different results with different keywords. Let me give you an example of how to search for a transfer.

If you type into Google keywords like "How to find transfer bus from Dalaman airport to Oludeniz," Google will display multiple pages with various transfer options. Several pages load with many recommendations. Go through the offered options and choose the one that suits you best. In my case in Oludeniz, these were the options:

1. The hotel offered me a transfer from the airport to the hotel and back for 120 euros.

2. Another option was to take a shuttle bus from the airport to the hotel for a similar price.

3. Take a city bus to Fethiye, then a taxi from Fethiye to Oludeniz.

4. Take a taxi directly from Dalaman airport to Oludeniz.

5. The last option I found online was to take the Otokar bus to Fethiye, then a minibus from Fethiye to Oludeniz.

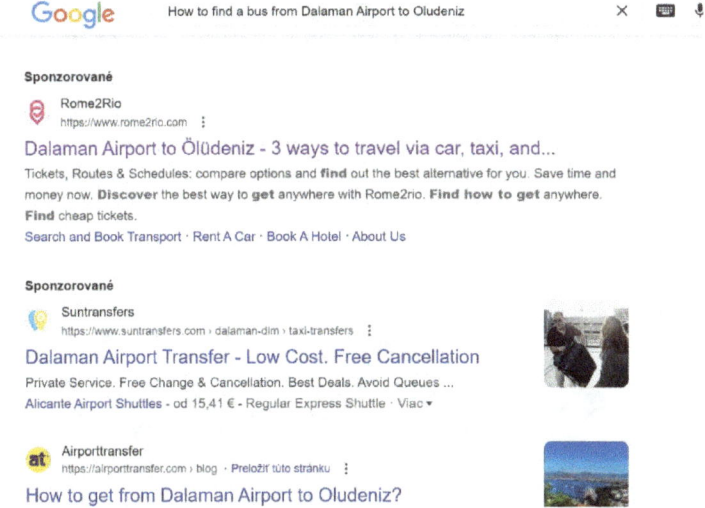

I chose the last (5th) option, and the entire trip cost me 3.73 euros. This method allows you to find any transfer using keywords.

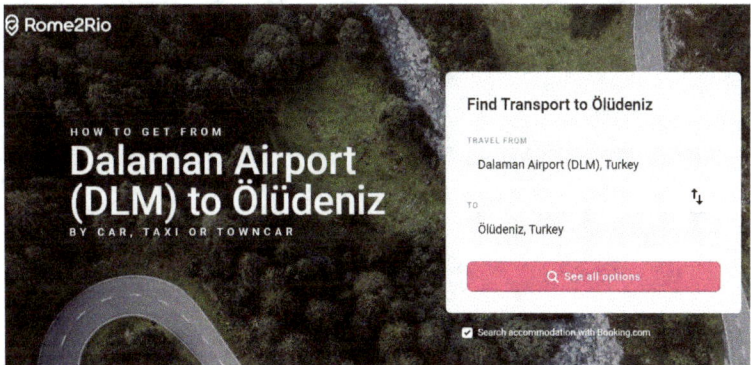

Tip: Based on price and comfort, choose the transfer that suits you best. I traveled by city bus and saved a significant amount. This search method is universal and can be used to find transfers from airports anywhere in the world. Just look at the different options and pick the one most convenient or economical for you.

Chapter 7

TRIP.COM – SEARCH ENGINE FOR TRIPS AND ATTRACTIONS NEARBY

If you want to discover the most interesting places around you during your travels and vacations — from famous landmarks to lesser-known but magical spots — the Trip.com portal is a great helper. Just enter the name of the destination (e.g., "Barcelona" or "Ölüdeniz"), and Trip.com will offer you:

- The most popular attractions nearby,
- Ratings from other travelers,
- Tips for tours, tickets, and advantageous packages,
- Even lesser-known local experiences you might otherwise miss.

It's a practical assistant for planning — whether you want to visit historical monuments, natural beauties, or fun places for the family. Additionally, it often allows you to book tickets in advance, saving you time and stress. Click on "Attractions and Tours" in the menu at the top right or on the left side menu, and Trip.com will show you discounted tickets for attractions nearby.

Fethiye Paragliding ♡

🔥 7,2 ⓘ 4,9 / 71 Bewertungen ›

● Geöffnet Fethiye Paragliding: Öffnungszeiten ›
Altersanforderungen | + 3 weitere

ⓘ **Empfohlene Besuchszeit:** 1-2 Stunde   ● **Adresse:** Ovacık, Güneş Otel Yanı, Ölüdeniz Cd No:31, 48300 Fethiye/M

📞 **Telefon:** Telefonnummer der Attraktion: +90 541 107 48 00

Fethiye Paragliding: Bewertungen anderer Besucher
🙂 Was Here! 5️⃣ Outstanding

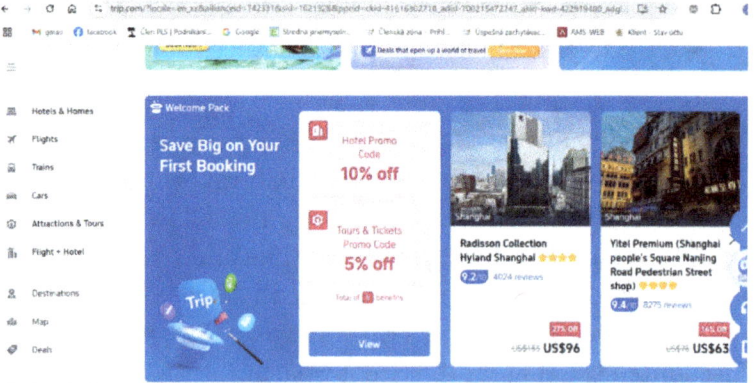

Tip: It's great to use Trip.com after arriving at your destination. It shows you currently available attractions based on your location, along with discounts that are available at that moment.

Trip to Turkey — Ölüdeniz

Some time ago, I visited Turkey, specifically the region southwest of Antalya. I arrived in Dalaman, heading to Ölüdeniz. Ölüdeniz is a small seaside resort in the Muğla region, located where the Aegean and Mediterranean seas meet.

Turkish Ölüdeniz is truly a beautiful place, about 75 km from the town of Dalaman, where the airport is located. If you are looking for a region that combines stunning nature, crystal-clear sea, and a touch of history, you definitely won't be disappointed when you come here.

Not far from Ölüdeniz is the town of Fethiye, a well-known traditional Turkish harbor and market town, reachable by a 15-minute ride on the Otokar bus.

Chapter 8

FLIGHT FROM BRATISLAVA TO DALAMAN, TURKEY

The flight from Bratislava to Dalaman took just under two and a half hours. The atmosphere at the airport was calm and pleasant, exactly as I had imagined at the start of my holiday, determined to have wonderful experiences.

Upon arrival in Dalaman, the weather was still beautifully warm. The journey from the airport to Fethiye was comfortable and quick, and once we arrived, we immediately started exploring the charming town. After arriving, we enjoyed a fantastic dinner and a refreshing Efes beer, which we savoured and which perfectly refreshed us. The day ended with a well-deserved rest.

The next morning, we enjoyed a delicious breakfast and unforgettable Turkish coffee at a local restaurant. They say Turkish hospitality warms your heart, which is why Ölüdeniz is definitely a place you should add to your travel list.

Interesting places in and around Ölüdeniz include:

1. **Butterfly Valley (Kelebekler Vadisi)** – one of the few places where the untouched nature of Ölüdeniz is preserved. At first glance, Butterfly Valley amazes you and is rightly considered a true paradise for nature lovers.
2. **Kumburnu Beach**, with its crystal-clear water, is also a must-see. I believe you will want to visit this natural reserve located in the Blue Lagoon.
3. **Lycian Way** – an ancient path with beautiful views.
4. **Babadag** – a mountain with a magnificent sea view.
5. **Belcekiz** – a beautiful beach with crystal-clear water.
6. **Ölüdeniz Nature Park** – a park with stunning nature and beautiful vistas.
7. **Ölüdeniz Kidrak Bay** – a lovely bay with crystal-clear water and white sand.
8. **Kabak Bay** – a bay with beautiful beaches and breathtaking views.

9. **Teleferik Cable Car** – leads up to 1900 m above sea level; a launch ramp for paragliding.

Ölüdeniz Resort and Paragliding

Paragliding is a popular activity in the Ölüdeniz area, launching from the nearby Babadag mountain. It's considered one of the most unforgettable experiences since it involves tandem flying from the summit of Babadag.

All these amazing places, plus the sea view from Babadag mountain—especially magical at sunset—are definitely worth seeing. If you try paragliding from Babadag, this experience and the view will stay with you forever in your memories.

Paragliding from 2000 meters above sea level is truly an experience worth having. The cable car (Teleferik) will take you up for 10 euros per person. First, you go by gondola to 1700 meters, then continue by chairlift to the summit.

Once you reach the final station, the view will take your breath away. The stunning vistas of Ölüdeniz and its coastline are simply breathtaking.

If you want even more adrenaline, your experienced pilot can take you higher and perform some acrobatic maneuvers right on the parachute. It's a thrilling experience that fills you with a sense of freedom and joy in every moment.

During the flight, you'll see the dazzlingly clear sea, beaches, and cliffs from 2000 meters above. After the flight, instructors professionally prepare videos and photos so you can keep memories of this amazing day.

On the beach, besides watching the flying and landing paragliders, you can relax at one of the snack bars near the cable car stations—an ideal chance to enjoy a refreshing drink, admire the beautiful surroundings, and watch visitors participate in this heavenly adventure or even join tandem flying yourself.

The flight price ranges from 65 to 75 euros per person, depending on the provider. This experience is guaranteed to delight you—the flight along the entire coastline offers an incomparable view from above that will literally take your breath away.

Turkish Cuisine

Turkish food is truly fascinating, and if you're a lover of good meals, you will definitely enjoy it here. Every dish in Turkey is full of natural flavors and aromas, resulting from a blend of Mediterranean, Middle Eastern, and Asian influences. All ingredients are fresh, which makes the food even more delicious.

Let's start with breakfast, which in Turkey is not just a quick cup of coffee but a real culinary experience. On the table, you'll find various types of cheese (don't forget the famous beyaz peynir – white cheese), fresh vegetable salads, olives, honey, fresh breads, and also tasty omelets and eggs prepared just the way you like them—from soft to hard. And speaking of eggs, be sure to try Menemen – a wonderful mix of eggs, tomatoes, peppers, and spices, served with fresh bread.

When it comes to lunch and dinner, you're in the right place in Turkey. Turkish cuisine is known for its grilled dishes. Here, kebab deserves a special mention—you definitely shouldn't miss trying it in its homeland. Whether it's şavarma (grilled meat cubes) or dürüm (kebab wrapped in pita bread), it always tastes fantastic. Be sure to order a glass of ayran (a yogurt-based drink), which is excellent for refreshing yourself after a meal.

Other specialties you simply must try are Meze—various small appetizers perfect for trying different flavors. Popular choices include stuffed grape leaves, and different kinds of dips like hummus (chickpea dip), baba ganoush (eggplant dip), and tabbouleh (a fresh salad with bulgur and herbs).

Another irresistible classic is Turkish Dolma—stuffed grape leaves (or vegetables) filled with rice, meat, or a combination of both. And if you want something truly tasty and unique, try lahmacun, a thin, crispy pizza topped with a spicy meat and vegetable base. These dishes are great for a light snack during the day or as starters before your main course.

And what would a visit to Turkey be without baklava—a sweet treat known worldwide? This sweet, nutty delicacy is made with thin layers of phyllo dough and beautifully sweetened with honey. If you're looking for something even sweeter, don't miss Lokum, also known as Turkish delight—a gelatinous candy flavored with rose, citrus, and other delightful tastes.

Turkey is also home to wonderful vegetable dishes such as Imambayildi (eggplant stuffed with garlic and tomatoes), Kisir (a bulgur salad with vegetables), and freshly made Pide (Turkish flatbread pizza), which can be filled with various meat or vegetarian ingredients.

Finally, don't forget the local coffee—strong, aromatic, and the perfect way to end your meal. Drinking coffee in

Turkey is a tradition, and its preparation is truly special. And if you have a sweet tooth, after coffee be sure to try a Turkish dessert like künefe—a sweet treat made from thin noodles filled with cheese and soaked in honey.

Turkish cuisine is truly unique and diverse, ranging from light dishes to rich and spicy meals. Whether you choose street food from a bustling alley or dine in an elegant restaurant, you can always look forward to excellent food that will completely captivate you.

On holiday in Ölüdeniz, it's a whole different experience than at home—no obligations, just relaxation and enjoying every moment. Let yourself be pampered, served, and simply savour every moment. You'll be completely absorbed in tasting local specialties, swimming in the beautiful sea, and trying various sports and excursion activities.

The Beach in Ölüdeniz

The beach is long, pebbly, and surrounded by beautiful natural scenery. It's the perfect spot to relax under the umbrellas, which are conveniently spaced along the entire shore. Throughout the day, you can unwind on sunbeds available for rent at a price of 10.48 euros per day. At the same time, you can enjoy the stunning view of the bay and the excursion boats that regularly dock here.

    If you decide to visit the nearby Blue Lagoon, a nature reserve, you'll enjoy the experience even more. This area is a bit pricier—sunbeds with umbrellas here cost about 12.48 euros. But the Blue Lagoon is definitely worth seeing. It's an ideal place for families with children, thanks to its sandy beach adapted for the little ones. Of course, there are a few more people and a livelier atmosphere, but that's all part of the wonderful holiday vibe.

When it comes to convenience, both the Blue Lagoon and Ölüdeniz are really well equipped. Payment terminals for card transactions are available everywhere on and around the beach, so you don't have to worry about finding an exchange office. Payments are simple, and the exchange rate is calculated directly by your bank. Every few steps, you'll find a beach bar offering fresh food, seafood, wraps, burgers, and of course, cold drinks and ice cream. The waiters are very friendly and will happily bring your order straight to your sunbed, so you don't have to worry about a thing—relax and enjoy if that's your style.

You'll also find toilets, showers, and changing rooms on the beach—everything is close at hand so you can enjoy your holiday without any worries. Overall, the beach and its surroundings are excellently equipped, with everything you need easily accessible, encouraging you to savor every single minute here.

Trips

Trips in Ölüdeniz are a truly memorable experience, full of unforgettable moments. Let's start with a boat cruise. All excursion boats depart from the harbor in Ölüdeniz with a lively atmosphere and loud music that immediately pulls you into the summer rhythm. The boat sets off every day between 10:30 and 11:00 AM and returns around 5:00 PM in the afternoon. During this full-day cruise, you'll visit stunning places like Butterfly Valley and Gemiler Island. It's a truly unique experience — 35 euros per person includes not only the amazing cruise but also a delicious grilled lunch right on board and convenient transfers from and back to your hotel. Unforgettable scenery, crystal-clear water, and refreshing breeze add to the magic of the summer atmosphere on the boat.

Another fantastic trip is the journey to the Turtle Beach in Dalyan. This trip takes you to one of the most beautiful places where sea turtles and their nests are carefully protected. Besides this amazing site, you can enjoy swimming in clean waters and relaxing in the mud baths, which have beneficial effects on your skin. This trip, priced at 167 euros per person, is truly unforgettable, combining natural beauty with relaxation and adventure.

Each of these trips offers a completely new perspective on Turkey. You'll fall in love with the beauty of nature, history, and culture. The cruise, relaxation, and fun blend seamlessly, so you'll enjoy every second, and the experiences will fill you with positive energy and joy.

The Sea in Ölüdeniz

The water is not only beautifully clear but also pleasantly warm — with a temperature of 29°C, it refreshes and gently warms you at the same time. When you lie on the surface, the sea gently carries you on its sparkling waves, and you just let yourself be pampered by this amazing experience, which is absolutely fantastic. While swimming, I enjoyed watching the sea life below me. I saw small black fish swimming in schools around and beneath me, peacefully in harmony with nature. The seabed was sandy, occasionally dotted with rocks. I also admired sea urchins — though I admit only from a safe distance. One brave one was even on land, so I could take a close look at it. My first day on the beach in Ölüdeniz was relaxed — spending the whole day soaking up the sun. Always in the shade, but even so, I returned home beautifully bronzed. The following days were filled with adventure as well. Every day brought something new — trips, water fun, sports activities… and lots of laughter. The days were packed with programs and joy, and in the evenings, we took walks along the sea, tasted delicious food, and planned the next adventures. It was a great trip and vacation; whenever I think back on it, I feel joy and immediately smile.

Now it's your turn.

Open your diary and start planning your travel adventure right now! ☐✈

☝ Here you'll find a short worksheet: Travel Plan and Practical Traveler's Plan, which will help you organize your dream vacation step by step. Fill out the attachments carefully, and your trip begins.

Travel Plan – jot it down 😊

📍 My destination: mountains, sea, cities, countryside?
....

🐾 Where will I travel? ... choose countries
....

✈ Flights – skyscanner.com, momondo.com, kiwi.com
....

♡ Insurance – Union, Uniqa, AXA, or through your payment card ....

🛏 Accommodation – booking.com, hotels.com, tripadvisor.com ....

🍽 Meals – breakfast, half board, all inclusive, or local restaurants ....

🚐 Airport transfer – public transport, shuttle bus, taxi, car rental ....

🚲 Getting around – bus, taxi, scooter, bike
....

🗡 Trips and attractions nearby – tickets can also be bought online ....

🎁 Gifts and other expenses – don't forget souvenirs like Turkish honey, baklava, coffee ....

Practical Traveller's Plan

1. Before Departure

- **Destination:** [Enter country/city name]
- **Travel dates:** From [Date] to [Date]
- **Travel insurance:** Obtain coverage for your international trip
    - Insurance company contact: ...
    - Phone number: ...
    - Email: ...
- **Documents:**
    - Passport (check validity – must be valid at least 6 months after your return)
    - Visa (if required) and national ID card (if traveling within the EU)
- **Document copies:** Make photocopies or scans of your passport, visa and tickets; save them to the cloud or keep physical copies

2. Travel Itinerary

- **Flights / Transportation:**
    - Departure: [Airport/Station], [Time]

- Arrival: [Airport/Station], [Time]
- Booking reference: [Reservation number, airline contact details]
- **Accommodation:**
  - Hotel/Hostel/Airbnb: [Name of accommodation]
  - Address: [Full address]
  - Check-in: [Time] / Check-out: [Time]
  - Reception contact: [Phone number]
- **Local transportation:**
  - Airport transfer: [Taxi/shuttle, time]
  - Public transport: Bus/metro info (download map or app)

Packing Checklist

(Verify before you leave)

- **Clothing:** According to weather (warm layers / light clothing, swimwear, hiking boots, socks, underwear, T-shirts, trousers, shirts, dresses)
- **Travel documents:** Passport, ID card, tickets
- **Electronics:** Phone, charger, power adaptor, power bank
- **First-aid kit:** Motion-sickness pills, pain relief, basic supplies, disinfectant
- **Toiletries:** Toothbrush, toothpaste, sunscreen, insect repellent, deodorant
- **Accessories:** Sunglasses, hat, map, guidebook

4. Safety Measures

- **Embassy contacts:** [Phone and address of your country's embassy in the destination]
- **Local emergency number:** [112 or other local equivalent]
- **Securing valuables:** Use the hotel safe; don't carry all your documents or cash in one place

- **Contact list backup:** Keep a list of key contacts (family, friends) stored in your phone

5. Daily Itinerary

Day 1:

- Morning activity: [e.g. city tour]
- Lunch: [Restaurant name, address]
- Afternoon: [Activity, e.g. museum visit or beach]
- Dinner: [Restaurant name, address]

Day 2:

- Morning activity: [Hiking or sightseeing]
- Lunch: [Restaurant name, address]
- Afternoon: [Shopping or free time]
- *Repeat for each subsequent day as needed*

6. Finances – Budget

- Accommodation: [Amount]
- Food: [Amount per day]
- Transportation: [Amount]
- Activities: [Amount]
- **Payment methods:** Bring a payment card and local-currency cash; always have emergency cash on hand

7. Return Home

- **Document check:** Before heading to the airport/station, confirm your passport remains valid at least 6 months after your return
- **Transport to airport:** Pre-book a transfer or arrange a taxi via the hotel
- **Hotel check-out:** [Time/Details]
- **Flight home:** Verify flight number and departure time

8. After You Return

- Review all documents and confirm any credit-card charges
- Share your experiences with friends or record them in your travel journal

Preparations & Contact:
anna.cestovanie@gmail.com

www.a-medial.sk

Traveler's Checklist: Packing Like a Pro

Clothing

- 3–4 tops (a mix of comfortable and dressy)
- 2 pairs of pants —or 1 pair of pants + 1 skirt or dress
- 1 lightweight blazer or jacket
- 1 versatile evening dress
- Sleepwear
- Underwear (at least 7 pieces)
- 1 swimsuit
- 1 scarf or shawl

Shoes

- 1 comfortable pair for walking
- 1 stylish pair for evenings
- (Optional) lightweight flip-flops or sandals

Toiletries (travel sizes or solids)

- Toothbrush + toothpaste
- Moisturiser + sunscreen
- Shampoo + conditioner
- Comb or brush
- Basic makeup

- Feminine hygiene products

Documents & Personal Items

- Passport / national ID
- Travel insurance
- Phone + charger
- Universal adapter
- Booking confirmations (digital and printed)
- Money / cards / local currency

Health & Safety

- Daily medications + a little extra
- Small first-aid kit (bandages, pain reliever, disinfectant)
- Respirator / masks (if needed)
- Mini antibacterial gel

Accessories

- Sunglasses
1. Hat / cap
2. Collapsible water bottle
- Notebook + pen
- Book / e-reader
- Headphones
- 1 lightweight day-bag (canvas or foldable)

Conclusion

Dear travellers in soul and heart,
In this e-book, *How to Travel Effectively and Joyfully*, I have lovingly shared with you tips, tricks, and little secrets that can make your travels more enjoyable and easier. I hope you've found not only useful advice but also a spark of inspiration to encourage you to set off on your next adventures.

The world is vast, diverse, and beautiful — just waiting for you to step into it. Set your goal, let your dreams carry you, and start planning. Your story can begin today.

At the very end of this book, you will find a practical worksheet that you can fill out to take your first concrete step toward your next journey. Allow your plans to turn into memories that you will look back on with a smile for years to come.

If this e-book has pleased you or brought you something useful, I would be very happy if you shared it with me and proudly showed me your travel plan that you've created.

Write to me at: anna.cestovanie@gmail.com — every comment, question, or feedback is a gift to me.

May your next trip be filled with joy, peace, and little miracles at every step.
And don't forget — the most beautiful journey is the one you create yourself.

With enthusiasm and respect,
Anna.

About the Author

My name is Anna Imrichová and I love discovering the world – with an open heart, curiosity, and joy. After years in advertising, media, and creative projects, I decided to distill my travel experiences into a book that might inspire even those who hesitate to embark on their own adventure. In my life, I have pursued various professions – from teaching and education, which taught me patience, to working in television, creating ad campaigns, and writing projects focused on sports and senior education. I am the author of the book "Management" and with enthusiasm I have also created several songs—lyrics and music—that express my passion for creativity and emotion.

My heart belongs especially to travel, nature, music, photography, reading motivational literature, and creation – from words to images. I believe that travel is not just about places, but about inner growth, peace, and inspiration.
If my book encourages you, delights you, or brings you one step closer to your own travel dreams, it will have fulfilled its purpose.

I welcome you to my social media, where you'll find more inspiration and personal insights:
Email: anna.cestovanie@gmail.com
Instagram: @anna.imrichova
Facebook: https://www.facebook.com/anna.imrichova
Website: www.a-medial.sk

Explore More on My Website

Dear Reader,

Thank you for reading this book! If you'd like some personalized advice on how to travel more effectively, feel free to scan the QR code to contact me directly. I'll get back to you within 24–48 hours and help you plan your next adventure!

www.ingramcontent.com/pod-product-compliance
Lightning Source LLC
Chambersburg PA
CBHW052107070526
44584CB00017B/2377